GUINEA PIGS

By Slim Goodbody

Illustrations: Ben McGinnis

Consultant: Kate Bergen Pierce,
Doctor of Veterinary Medicine

Gareth Stevens
Publishing

Dedication: To my friend Richard Stegman — thanks for twenty years of travel and inspiration

Please visit our web site at: www.garethstevens.com
For a free color catalog describing Gareth Stevens Publishing's list
of high-quality books, call 1-800-542-2595 (USA) or 1-800-387-3178 (Canada).
Gareth Stevens Publishing's fax: 1-877-542-2596

Library of Congress Cataloging-in-Publication Data

Burstein, John.
    Guinea pigs / John Burstein.
      p. cm. — (Slim Goodbody's inside guide to pets)
    Includes bibliographical references and index.
    ISBN-10 0-8368-8957-6   ISBN-13: 978-0-8368-8957-4 (lib. bdg.)
    1. Guinea pigs as pets—Juvenile literature. I. Title.
  SF459.G9B85 2008
  636.935'92—dc22
                                 2007033459

This edition first published in 2008 by
Gareth Stevens Publishing
A Weekly Reader® Company
1 Reader's Digest Road
Pleasantville, NY 10570-7000 USA

Photos: All photos from iStock Photos except page 8 (top left) courtesy of David L. Dyer
Illustrations: Ben McGinnis, Adventure Advertising

Managing Editor: Valerie J. Weber, Wordsmith Ink
Designer: Tammy West, Westgraphix LLC
Gareth Stevens Senior Managing Editor: Lisa M. Guidone
Gareth Stevens Creative Director: Lisa Donovan

Printed in the United States of America

1 2 3 4 5 6 7 8 9 10 10 09 08

CONTENTS

Words that appear in the glossary are printed in **boldface** type the first time they occur in the text.

GREETINGS, PIG PALS

Hello! My name is Squeakers, and I am a guinea pig. Small and soft, I am nice to hold. My human family thinks I am very cute.

Guinea pigs are favorite pets for families around the world. It's easy to see why. We love to cuddle. We are easy to care for. We hardly ever get sick. We rarely bite or scratch.

I think guinea pigs make the greatest pets in the world. We eat less than rabbits do. We're friendlier than most cats. We don't need as much attention as dogs. We aren't as noisy as birds. We're easier to handle than hamsters or gerbils. We're much more playful than fish.

FUN FACT

Guinea pigs have been popular pets for more than four hundred years! Queen Elizabeth I of England owned a pet guinea pig way back in the 1600s.

When a guinea pig first meets you, she may act a bit afraid and shy. Once she feels safe, however, she will be very friendly. She may even learn to come when you call.

Guinea pigs are *herd* animals. That term means that when we lived in the wild, we lived in groups of ten to twenty animals. Now that we are pets, we like to think of our owners as members of our herd.

Squeaker Says

Guinea pigs like company. Two guinea pigs in the house are usually happier than one. Just make sure their cage is nice and roomy.

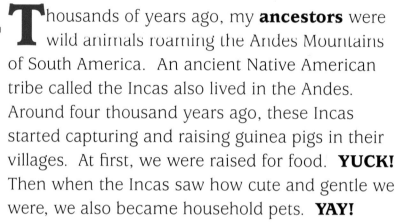

Thousands of years ago, my **ancestors** were wild animals roaming the Andes Mountains of South America. An ancient Native American tribe called the Incas also lived in the Andes. Around four thousand years ago, these Incas started capturing and raising guinea pigs in their villages. At first, we were raised for food. **YUCK!** Then when the Incas saw how cute and gentle we were, we also became household pets. **YAY!**

The Incas also used us for healing. If somebody was sick, an Incan healer rubbed a guinea pig over the body of a sick person. When it started to squeak, the healer believed it was telling the exact place where the problem was! The Incas believed that black guinea pigs were the most special of all. In the wild, few guinea pigs were black.

NORTH
AMERICA

ANDES
MOUNTAINS

SOUTH
AMERICA

ANDES MOUNTAINS

During the 1500s, Dutch sailors first brought guinea pigs to Europe from South America. About two hundred years later, guinea pigs arrived in the United States.

A Pig Mystery

No one actually knows why we are called guinea pigs. We are not from the country of Guinea in Africa, and we are not pigs! Some people think we got part of our name because the Dutch sailors may have stopped off in Guinea before they reached Europe. People in Europe may have thought that Guinea was our **homeland**.

Part of our name may come from the fact that we are built a little bit like pigs. We have large heads, thick necks, plump bodies, and almost no tails. We make noises that are a little like the sounds pigs make. We also spend a lot of time eating. **YUM!**

Squeakers Says

Keep your pet guinea pig inside. Be sure he stays warm during the winter and cool in the summer. Keep him in a room where your family spends lots of time, so he has plenty of company.

GREAT SHAPE

Guinea pigs have a lot more bones than humans.

Adult humans have 206 bones. Grown-up guinea pigs have 258 bones.

I have thirty-four bones in my spine, forty-three bones in each front leg, thirty-six bones in each back leg, and twenty-six rib bones. The rest of my bones are in my skull, breastbone, and tail.

My skull protects my brain. My skull is big, so I have plenty of room for my big, strong teeth.

A Big-Bellied Build

I also have a big belly that almost hides my back legs. My stomach is so big that my back legs have to point sideways to fit around it!

I have short leg bones and a short neck. This body plan means my mouth stays close to the ground. I do not have to bend down very far to pick up food. You could say I am well built — for feeding!

FUN FACT
My seven tail bones are tiny. They are placed so close to my bottom that you cannot see my tail from the outside.

Squeakers Says

Your guinea pig's bones can break easily if you drop her. Please be sure to hold and carry her carefully. When you pick her up, use two hands! Slide one hand under her whole body, and put your other hand over her to keep her steady. Always support her weight firmly and move slowly.

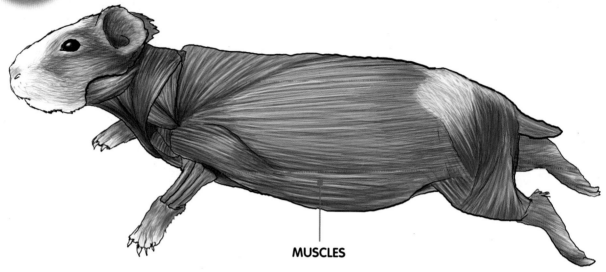

MUSCLES

You probably started running when you were two or three years old. I could run when I was only two or three hours old!

Guinea pigs are fast. We needed speed when we lived in the wild. After all, we had to escape from animals who wanted to eat us. We stayed ahead of them by ducking through thick brushes and racing around sharp turns.

Dawn and dusk were the safest feeding times for wild guinea pigs. At those times of day, our **predators** had a hard time spotting us. We would run from cover, grab some food, and race back to safety. We're still more active in the morning and evening.

FUN FACT

If I don't have time to run from danger, I will be tricky. I will not move a muscle. I will play dead, hoping that I will not be noticed.

Not Ready for the Olympics

I am sorry to say that guinea pigs are not great athletes. For example, we cannot climb like squirrels. Guinea pigs are not great hunters, either. It does not take a lot of skill to sneak up on a blade of grass. Our jaw muscles are strong, however, because our food can be very tough. Our neck muscles are strong, too, because they must lift our heavy heads.

I cannot leap very far, but when I am happy, I like to jump up and down. I throw my hind legs up in the air and leap around like crazy. This movement is called *popcorning* because I look like corn being popped.

Squeakers Says

Your guinea pig needs exercise every day just like you do. Let him loose on a clean, bare floor, and watch him go for an hour. You can give him some toys to play with such as old socks, shoeboxes, paper bags, and empty toilet paper rolls.

Your hands and feet have the same number of fingers and toes. My front feet and back feet are different. My front feet each have four toes. My back feet each have three toes.

All four of my feet have tough pads of skin covering the soles. These pads help protect my toe bones.

All four feet have sharp toenails called claws. Claws are made from the same material as your fingernails. Some of my nails grow straight, and others curl a bit.

Nonstop Nails

My toenails never stop growing! About every month, I need to have them clipped. If my nails grow too long, I'll have problems. I won't be able to walk well. My nails may get torn or broken, which can lead to an **infection**. My feet will get sore.

When guinea pigs lived in the wild, they never worried about the length of their nails. Running on rough ground and stones would naturally wear their nails down to the right length.

Squeakers Says

Be careful when you clip your guinea pig's toenails. It is easy to cut too much. Children should not do the clipping. Adults should check with the **vet** to find out how to trim nails safely.

TERRIFIC TEETH

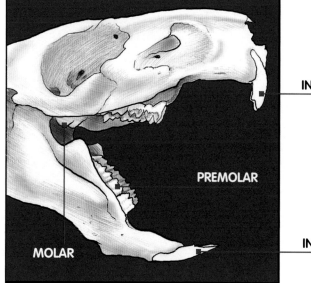

INCISOR

PREMOLAR

INCISOR

MOLAR

HUMAN TEETH

I have two upper lips and one bottom lip. You can only see four teeth behind my lips, but I have twenty white teeth in all. I have four incisors in front — two on top and two on the bottom. My incisors are sharp. I use them for gnawing and biting. The rest of my teeth are flatter. They are in the back of my mouth and are called premolars and molars. They grind up my food.

When I was born, all my adult teeth were in place except my back molars. In a short time, these molars grew in as well. Humans don't get all their adult teeth until they are twelve or thirteen years old!

Not only that, but my teeth never, ever stop growing. I have to keep wearing them down by gnawing and chewing. Otherwise, my teeth could grow so long that I wouldn't be able to eat! To keep my teeth trimmed, I eat tough foods like hay, lettuce, and carrots. Chewing these tough foods helps grind down my teeth.

Squeakers Says
Gnawing on a piece of wood will help keep your guinea pig's teeth trim. Some kinds of wood aren't good for your pet, so check with your vet about what kind of wood to use. Guinea pigs love to gnaw. If you leave this book near a guinea pig, don't be surprised if she takes a bite!

Some guinea pigs have long hair, some have medium-length hair, and some have short hair. Hair can be smooth and silky, but some can be shaggy, wiry, or rough. Some guinea pigs have crests of hair on the top of their heads or tufts of hair all over their body.

Some guinea pigs have a single solid color of hair. It can be gray, brown, white, or black. Others have a white band around their middle or spots. Some guinea pigs have three different colors of hair.

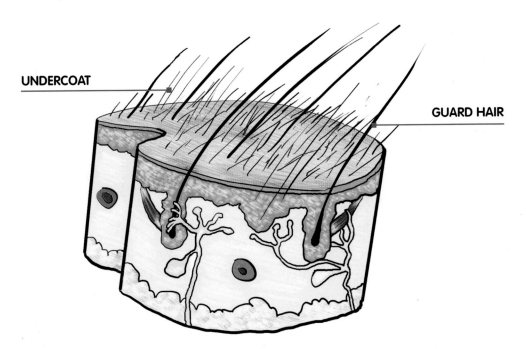
With a full coat of hair, I was a real little fur ball when I was born. My hair helps keep me warm and protected. Its color and pattern also helps me blend in with my **surroundings** and hide from enemies.

I have two kinds of hair. Close to my skin, I have a thick coat of short, soft hairs. Called an undercoat, these hairs help keep me warm. I have a second coat made up of longer hairs called guard hairs. Guard hairs protect my undercoat.

UNDERCOAT

GUARD HAIR

Squeakers Says

Your guinea pig needs a good brushing every day. He gets dirt and food hay stuck in his coat. Brushing keeps his hair clean and free of snarls. It also helps remove loose hair. Be sure to use a soft brush. If the bristles are too hard, they can scratch his skin.

17

I love to eat! I can't think of anything I like to do more! I eat small amounts of food all day long. I spend about six hours each day filling my belly.

I live on grasses and other plants. I love lots of different fruits and vegetables, such as carrots, green beans, lettuce, apples, and pears.

Some of these foods are hard to break down and **digest**. When I eat them, I am only able to get some of the energy I need from them. Then I poop out the food in soft clumps.

Eating Poop Is Not Gross!

These clumps have lots of **nutrients**, so I eat them. That way, I can get the rest of the energy from these foods. In other words, the food passes through me twice. Double **digestion** helps me get the most nutrients from the food I eat.

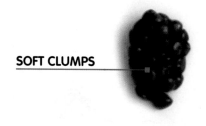

SOFT CLUMPS

POOP

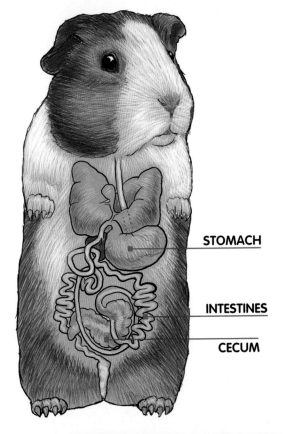

STOMACH

INTESTINES

CECUM

After I swallow the clumps, they go to an **organ** called the cecum. The cecum is a part of my **intestines**. After my food is digested a second time in the cecum, I poop it out again. I do not eat the second kind of poop.

Pigs, People, and Vitamin C

Almost all animals in the world can make vitamin C in their bodies. Human beings and guinea pigs can't, however. To stay healthy, we need foods with vitamin C, such as cauliflower, broccoli, and kale. I can also get vitamin C in guinea pig food pellets.

I also need to drink lots of fresh water every day. My owner changes my water bottle every morning.

Squeakers Says

Be sure to wash your guinea pig's fruits and vegetables. Dirty food can make her sick. Also, do not feed her rhubarb, beans, or potatoes with green spots. These vegetables are all poisonous to her! Don't feed her dairy products, either. They can upset her stomach.

I love to talk. I do not speak English, of course, but I make lots of different sounds that mean different things. My sounds tell my owner and other guinea pigs how I feel. Not all guinea pigs make every sound, but here is a list of the sounds I make:

Wheek This loud noise sounds just like it is spelled. It means that I am excited. It can mean "feed me," "pay attention to me," or "I need help!"

Purr I make this sound when I am happy. I purr when I am being held nicely and petted or when I get a special treat.

Chut I make this sound when I am chasing something.

Whine I make this sound when I am being chased.

BEWARE OF **GUINEA PIG**

Rumble This sound is usually a warning. I use it to say that I'm hearing something I do not like.

Chatter I make this sound by gnashing my teeth together. It is a warning to others to keep away. When I chatter, I raise my head so I look more dangerous.

Chirp I make this sound when I am upset. It sounds almost like a bird.

Squeal or Shriek I make this loud, high sound when I am in pain or danger. I also use it when I am lonely or very afraid.

Squeakers Says

Your guinea pig gets scared of loud noises. He likes it when people speak in a soft voice. He doesn't like to hear a loud TV or loud music. Soft music can make him feel relaxed, however.

21

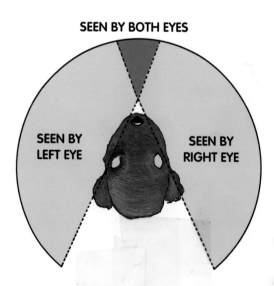

My big eyes are clear and bright and stick out slightly. They are on the sides of my head, giving me a wide range of vision. A wide range of vision means that I can see what is all around me without twisting my head around. I can see if somebody is creeping up from the side or from behind me. I can see if an owl is flying at me from above.

As long as something is moving, I can see it pretty easily. My eyes are not as good at spotting something that is keeping still, however. I guess that is because my safety depends more on seeing something attacking me than on something sitting still.

SEEN BY BOTH EYES

SEEN BY LEFT EYE

SEEN BY RIGHT EYE

When I look out at the world, I don't see as many colors as you do. Besides black and white, all I can see are blues, reds, and greens.

Where's My Food?

Here is a little secret I'll share with you. There is one major problem with having eyes on the side of my head. I cannot see the ground right under my nose! That means I can't see the food I am about to eat.

If you look closely, sometimes you will see a milky white fluid in my eyes. This fluid does not mean I have an eye infection. It just helps keep my eyes moist. I also spread it around to keep my face clean.

Squeakers Says

When you want to take your guinea pig out of her cage, let her know you're on your way. If she suddenly sees a giant hand reaching toward her, she can get frightened. Start humming sweetly, instead, and move very slowly as you head her way.

23

LISTEN HERE

My ears are flat, large, and thin. They usually hang down, but sometimes they lie open and flat against my head. They have little hairs inside to help stop dirt and germs from getting in.

Inside, my ears look a lot like yours. They have eardrums, **semicircular** canals, and **nerves** that carry messages to my brain.

My sense of hearing is excellent. I hate to brag, but my sense of hearing is better than yours. I can hear very high sounds that you cannot hear.

FUN FACT

My ears look a lot like tiny elephant ears.

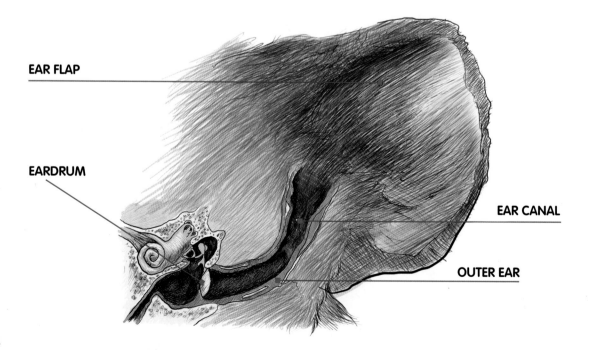

EAR FLAP

EARDRUM

EAR CANAL

OUTER EAR

I depend on my sense of hearing to keep me safe from danger. I may not be able to see something that is standing still or hiding, but I can hear it. I can hear supersoft sounds, like an animal brushing against some leaves.

I can tell different guinea pigs by the sounds they make. I can also tell the difference between the footsteps of my owner and the footsteps of other people. I can hear the refrigerator door open and know when food is coming.

Squeakers Says

Your guinea pig needs his ears checked once a week to be sure they look healthy. Please clean his ears every other week.

My nose is small, but my sense of smell is great! I can **detect** very slight odors in the air around me. My sense of smell is actually better than yours. I must admit, however, that dogs and cats have a better sense of smell than I do.

   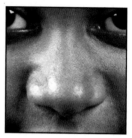

My sense of smell helps me in many ways. It helps me find food when I'm hungry. It helps me sniff out nearby dangers. It helps me make friends. When I meet another guinea pig for the first time, we usually touch noses or sniff just under each other's chin. It's a good way to find out about each other.

Whisker Width

Around my nose and mouth, I have a set of whiskers. They stick out to the sides and help me get around safely. The length of my whiskers tells me if I can fit though a space or not. Whiskers also help me find things in the dark. You may remember that I cannot see what is under my nose, so I depend upon my whiskers to feel my food.

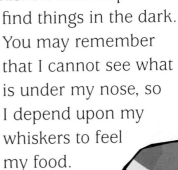

I would have to say that my sense of taste is OK but not great. I do like to taste all kinds of things. For example, I once chewed a hole in my owner's shirt!

Squeakers Says

Don't worry if you hear your guinea pig sneeze or cough once in a while. Some sneezing and coughing are normal for guinea pigs, just as they are for humans. If she sneezes and coughs a lot, however, or her nose starts running, you need to talk with a vet right away. Your guinea pig may have an infection and need medicine.

AMAZING FACTS

I hope you have enjoyed reading my book and learning about guinea pigs. If you are thinking about buying a guinea pig, you now know why we make such great pets. If you own a guinea pig, please give him or her a big kiss for me. Before I go, I think it would be fun to finish up with some more amazing guinea pig facts:

- The oldest guinea pig lived to be fifteen years old.

- Guinea pigs can have babies when they are about five weeks old. At that age, however, they are too young to make good parents.

- Guinea pigs were the first **rodents** to be tamed.

- Guinea pigs were one of the first small mammals to be sent into outer space.

- You can teach a guinea pig to waltz, jump, and turn in a circle.

- Guinea pigs start eating solid food when they are only two or three days old.

Guinea pigs have been known to eat bed sheets, clothing, shoelaces, newspapers, and even plastic.

In Peru, they keep about 65 million guinea pigs. Most will be eaten!

When guinea pigs are born, they weigh only about 3 ounces (85 grams).

If a guinea pig gets angry, its hair will stand on end. This makes it look bigger.

Guinea pigs have three eyelids. The third one cleans dust from their eyes when they blink.

Guinea pigs hardly ever need baths. Some are never bathed.

A more scientific word for guinea pig is *cavy*.

A male guinea pig is called a boar. A female guinea pig is called a sow. Baby guinea pigs are usually called pups.

GLOSSARY

ancestors — animals from whom an individual or group is descended

detect — to discover or find out information

digest — to break down food and change it into energy that the body needs to work

digestion — the process of breaking food down into a form that the body can use for energy

homeland — a country or area where someone was born or has a home

infection — a disease caused by germs or tiny animals

intestines — parts of the body through which food passes after it is eaten and leaves the stomach

nerves — special cells that join together and carry signals to and from the brain

nutrients — things needed by people, animals, and plants to live and grow

organ — a large part of the body, such as the heart, lungs, stomach, or liver, that does a specific job

predators — animals that hunt other animals for food

rodents — a group of animals with large front teeth for gnawing

semicircular — having a half-circle shape

surroundings — the area that an animal lives in

vet — short for *veterinarian*, a doctor who takes care of animals

FOR MORE INFORMATION

BOOKS

Getting to Know Your Guinea Pig. Children's Pet (series). Gill Page
   (Interpet Publishing)

Guinea Pigs. Pet Care (series). Bobbie Kalman and Kelley Macaulay
   (Crabtree Publishing)

My Guinea Pig and Me. For the Love of Animals (series). Immanuel
   Birmelin (Barron's Educational Series)

Pet Guinea Pigs. Pet Pals (series). Julia Barnes (Gareth Stevens Publishing)

The Wild Side of Pet Guinea Pigs. The Wild Side of Pets (series). Jo Waters
   (Raintree)

WEB SITES

Canny Cavies
www.oginet.com/Cavies
Check out this funny site and click on links to guinea pig movies and more.

Cavies Galore
www.caviesgalore.com/game
Play guinea pig games online and answer a quiz to test your knowledge of
guinea pig care.

Guinea Pig Care
www.aspca.org/site/PageServer?pagename = kids_pc_guinea_411
The American Society for the Prevention of Cruelty to Animals' Web site
has special pages just for learning about guinea pigs.

Your Guinea Pig
www.bbc.co.uk/cbbc/wild/pets/guineapig.shtml
Click on the interactive guide to learn more about guinea pigs..

Publisher's note to educators and parents: Our editors have carefully reviewed these Web sites to ensure
that they are suitable for children. Many Web sites change frequently, however, and we cannot guarantee
that a site's future contents will continue to meet our high standards of quality and educational value. Be
advised that children should be closely supervised whenever they access the Internet.

INDEX

Andes Mountains 6

babies 28, 29
baths 29
bones 8–9, 12
brains 8, 24
brushing 17

cages 5, 23
carrying 8
cecums 19

digestion 18–19

ears 24–25
eating 4, 7, 9, 10,
   15, 18, 19, 29
elephants 25
exercise 11
eyes 22–23, 29

feet 12
foods 9, 10, 11, 15,
   17, 18, 19, 23,
   25, 26, 27

hair 16–17, 29
hay 17, 19
heads 7, 11

healing 6
hearing 24–25
herds 5, 7
horses 19

Incas 6
infections 13, 23, 27
intestines 19

jaws 11

legs 8, 9, 11
lips 14

muscles 10–11
music 21

nails 12–13
names 7
necks 7, 11
noses 26–27
nutrients 18, 19

pigs 7
popcorning 11

running 10, 11, 13

scent 27
skin 12

skulls 8
sleeping 23
smelling 26
sounds 6, 7, 20–21
stomachs 9, 18, 19

tails 7, 8, 9
taste 27
teeth 8, 14–15, 21

vets 13, 15
vision 22, 23
vitamins 19

water 19
whiskers 27

ABOUT THE AUTHOR

John Burstein (also known as Slim Goodbody) has been entertaining and educating children for over thirty years. His programs have been broadcast on CBS, PBS, Nickelodeon, USA, and Discovery. He has won numerous awards including the Parent's Choice Award and the President's Council's Fitness Leader Award. Currently, Mr. Burstein tours the country with his multimedia live show "Bodyology." For more information, please visit slimgoodbody.com.